Mediterranean
Meal Plan

ek**1**

Lemon Ricotta Pancakes

Introduction

Welcome to your Mediterranean Meal Plan. This "Healthy Eating" program is based on the Mediterranean Diet and will help detox the body and achieve increased health and permanent weight loss.

We believe that optimal health can be achieved through preventative measures by eating a wide range of fresh "real" food, rich in nutrients, which is what the Mediterranean Diet is all about. The Mediterranean Diet is hailed by many health experts across the world as the most universally beneficial diet for long-term health. This way of eating not only promotes foods rich in Omega 3 and foods that are rich in fiber, vitamins, minerals and antioxidants (all of which promote good health), it is generally easy to follow without having to follow a set of strict rules like many other diets enforce.

We are so excited you are here and about to commence this 8-week program. You will eliminate the foods that cause many issues now and later in life, while focusing on nutrient-rich foods (typical of the Mediterranean Diet), which will support you living your best life.

While doing this program you will also develop health-promoting eating habits that provide the foundations for a life of vitality and longevity. Throughout this program you will see the emphasis is on eating plenty of plant-based foods, consisting of a wide variety of vegetables, herbs, some fruits, nuts, seeds and legumes. Red meat is limited to a serving or two a week, while you will have fish and poultry at least twice a week. Healthy fats are an important focus in the Mediterranean Diet and have been incorporated into most meals. We will discuss healthy fats in more detail in the coming weeks.

Before beginning this 8 week program, it is important that you take note of the following:

- Depending on what your current diet is like, (if you are eating a lot of processed foods), you may feel withdrawal symptoms such as headaches, nausea, weakness or tiredness for the first 2–7 days. This is your body ridding itself of stored toxins and it is important that you drink at least 3 liters (or 3/4 of a gallon) of water each day to support the elimination of these toxins.

- Whether you are cooking for just yourself or the whole family, ensure you plan ahead. Pay attention to the serving sizes of each recipe and adjust accordingly.

- Take stock of what you already have available at home and adjust your shopping list accordingly. Pick a day to go grocery shopping and then another for meal prep if you wish to prep food ahead of time. Buy only the foods you require for the week ahead and ensure you store them correctly. If possible, purchase your grains, legumes, nuts, seeds and other dry produce in bulk to cut costs. These items can also be stored in the freezer to extend shelf life.

- Follow the meal plans carefully. While each ingredient has been carefully planned to provide a balance of nutrients, recipes are also versatile. For example, feel free to make substitutions with ingredients you have on hand. You can swap feta with ricotta if that is what you have, or kale for spinach. Be sure to use whatever you have on hand before racing out to buy extra ingredients that may not be necessary.

- If you like to have a snack between meals, ensure you have whole, real food snacks. Some snack suggestions are vegetables sticks with hummus, olives, avocado on rice crackers, Greek yogurt with a piece of fresh fruit, or a small handful of mixed nuts and seeds.

- Do not skip meals. You should not feel hungry if you stick to the eating plan. If you skip a meal it may increase your hunger hormones and will be counterproductive. Also do your best to not eat anything after 7pm. This will help with your metabolism.

- Herbs are a wonderful source of nutrients and can assist with detoxification and achieving optimal health. Feel free to add a wide variety of fresh herbs (organic or home grown where possible) to your meals.

- Limit yourself to one mug of black coffee (with a dash of milk if you wish) per day with no sugar. You may have a glass or two of wine no more than three nights per week (opt for organic and preservative free).

- Other fluids that are allowed are green tea, herbal tea, fruit tea and freshly squeezed vegetable juices.

Golden Millet Porridge

This Week's Goal:

1. Get familiar with this week's recipes and the weeks ahead. Start to become familiar with the layout of each week's plan and what is required for prep.

2. Work out what your weekly routine is going to be like. What days are you going to do your inventory of foods and develop a shopping list? When will your shopping day be, and do you require a meal prep day? Set yourself up for success with a clear, organized plan.

Final Word:

Have fun! The most important part of this program is to enjoy it and have fun while doing it! Healthy eating is meant to be enjoyable, exciting and simple. There is no need to stress about it or make things too complicated. We suggest that you follow each week´s recipes as best you can and follow our outlined notes above with some basic rules, and you will be well on your way to a healthy eating regime that your body will not only thank you for, but which you can easily sustain for a lifetime.

Disclaimer:

The program is based on healthy eating and removing unhealthy foods. This program does not constitute medical advice. If you require advice in relation to any matter, you should consult an appropriate health professional. In particular, if you have a chronic disease or are on prescribed medication, check with your doctor before starting this program. Make sure you exclude any foods that you are allergic to.

Week 1			
Sunday	**Monday**	**Tuesday**	**Wednesday**
Lemon Ricotta Pancakes *(Page 36)* *(Be sure to prepare the ricotta cheese the night before as per recipe)*	Golden Millet Porridge *(Page 32)*	Fruit Salad with Italian Ricotta *(Page 30)*	Gourmet Feta Toast *(Page 34)* *(Substitute the Italian ricotta for the feta for as you will already have this on your grocery list. If you already have feta on hand feel free to use as per recipe)*
Spinach Torta *(Page 72)* *(Make double the serving size required and freeze leftovers for next week's Monday meal plan)*	Tuscan Tuna Salad *(Page 76)*	Falafels with Simple Greek Salad & Tahini Sauce *(Page 84)* *(Double the amount of falafels and tahini sauce required for meal. You will use these for dinner on Wednesday)*	Neapolitan Polenta Pie *(Page 94)* *(Make enough to have leftovers for Thursday's dinner)*
Meatloaf Stuffed with Proscuitto & Cheese *(Page 90)* Serve with Simple Greek Salad *(Page 54)*	Portuguese Chorizo Soup *(Page 98)* *(Make double the serving size required and freeze leftovers for next week's meal plan)*	Orange Baked Fish with Onions and Mushrooms *(Page 96)*	Leftover falafels *(Page 84)* Serve with Simple Greek Salad *(Page 54)* *(Use leftover falafels served alongside salad with tahini sauce to drizzle over instead of salad dressing)*

Notes:			
		The "Cheese" yogurt for tomorrow's Neapolitan Polenta Pie needs to be made at least 10–12 hours ahead of time. Prepare the yogurt tonight so it will be ready for tomorrow night's meal.	Tomorrow's chicken breast can be marinated overnight to save time the next day. Prepare them tonight so they are ready to cook for an easy lunch tomorrow.

Week 1

Thursday	Friday	Saturday
Fruit Salad with Italian Ricotta *(Page 30)*	Overnight Breakfast Strata *(Page 38)*	Stuffed Mushrooms *(Page 44)*
Simple Marinated Chicken Breast *(Page 70)* Serve with Simple Greek Salad *(Page 54)* *(Make enough extra chicken required to replace the turkey in Friday night's Turkey Barley Soup)*	Rice & Lentil Salad *(Page 62)*	Grilled Salmon on Herbed Couscous *(Page 64)*
Leftover Polenta Pie *(Page 94)*	Turkey Barley Soup *(Page 104)* *(Substitute the cooked turkey in this recipe with leftover cooked chicken breast)*	Roasted Lamb Rack with Velvet Black Olive Sauce *(Page 100)* *(Reserve the leftover roast lamb for next week's Saturday dinner meal plan. Store in an airtight container in the fridge)*

Notes:

Tomorrow night's dinner is a slow cooked recipe. Be sure to have all the ingredients prepared so you can easily throw it all in the slow cooker tomorrow morning.

Cook the rice for tomorrow's Rice and Lentil salad and store in an airtight container in the fridge. And, prepare the Overnight Breakfast Strata and place it in the fridge to be ready for cooking tomorrow.

It's Saturday night, treat yourself to a glass or two of wine and a square of dark chocolate.

WEEK 1 – Shopping List

Vegetables:
Arugala Leaves
Avocado
Baby Spinach Leaves
Bell Peppers
Black Ripe Olives
Butternut Squash
Capers
Carrots
Chives
Cucumber
Field Mushrooms
Frozen Spinach
Garlic
Garlic Clove
Green Bell Pepper
Mixed Lettuce
Mushrooms
Nicoise Olives
Olives
Onion
Pearl Onions
Portobello Mushrooms
Potatoes
Red Onion
Scallions
Stringed Green Beans
Yellow Bell Peppers
Zucchini

Fruit:
Apple
Cherry Tomatoes
Lemon
Nashi Pears
Pomegranate Arils
Tomatoes

Herbs:
Basil
Bay Leaf
Cilantro
Fennel Seed
Lemon Verbena
Mint
Oregano
Parsley

Rosemary Sprig
Thyme

Dairy:
Butter
Eggs
Feta
Greek Feta
Greek Yogurt
Italian Ricotta
Milk
Mozzarella Cheese
Parmesan Cheese
Ricotta Cheese

Bakery:
Bread Crumbs
Pie Crust
Sourdough Bread
Toast
Tortillas

Meat:
Chicken Breast
Chorizo Sausage
Flounder (Fish)
Ground Beef
Ground Pork
Lamb Racks
Prosciutto
Salmon Fillets
Turkey Breast

Other:
Chicken Stock
Couscous
Dried Italian Herbs
Dried Mustard
Flaxseed Sprouts
Honey
Lemon Juice
Millet
Orange Juice
Paprika
Pearl Barley
Pepitas
Pizza Sauce

Raisins
Rice
Vegetable Stock
Worcestershire Sauce

Check Your Pantry For The Following:
Baking Powder
Black Pepper
Black Pepper Corns
Canned Chickpeas
Canned Green Lentils
Canned Tomato Soup
Canned Tuna
Dijon Mustard
Dried Cranberries
Dried Majoram
Dried Oregano Leaves
Dried Porcini Mushrooms
Garlic Powder
Ground Cinnamon
Ground Cumin
Italian Dressing
Italian Dried Herbs
Olive Oil
Pimentos, Jar
Polenta
Prepared Mustard
Salt
Sea Salt
Sugar
Sundried Tomatoes
Tahini (Sesame Paste)
Walnuts
White Wine Vinegar
Whole Wheat Flour

Alcohol Used For Cooking:
Madeira Wine
White Wine

Spinach Torta

We

Mediterranean
Meal Plan

ek 2

Tortilla Española

Introduction

Welcome to Week 2 of your Mediterranean Meal Plan. We hope you are enjoying this healthy and delicious way of eating!

The diet, as you will begin to see, is all about fresh "real" food, with very limited processed foods. While doing this program, we want to teach you how to set yourself up to maintain this way of eating for good.

One of the best ways to reduce your consumption of processed foods and to eat a daily diet rich in nutrients is to ensure a well-stocked pantry full of single ingredients. Items such as ancient grains, beans, legumes, spices, nuts, seeds, healthy oils, and natural sweeteners such as raw honey are just a few ingredients to ensure become staples in your kitchen. From these kinds of individual ingredients, you can make an unlimited number of healthy meals that will not just taste amazing but also provide many nutritional benefits. When you have a good supply of quality healthy ingredients on hand it is so easy to be organized and stay committed to healthy eating.

To create a pantry stocked with health-promoting ingredients we suggest you just start one step at a time (there's no need to go and throw every item out of your kitchen that may not be that great)! Simply start replacing ingredients of concern (that may cause inflammation—more on that later) such as vegetable cooking oil with olive oil, and margarine with butter. Make one swap per week. You'll then have a pantry full of healthy alternatives in no time. Find below some of our top suggestions for easy "real-food" swaps that will go hand in hand with this Mediterranean meal plan.

Swap this for that:

Swap This:	For That:
Margarine, vegetable oil, canola oil, corn oil, soybean oil, ricebran oil	Extra virgin olive oil, coconut oil, ghee, butter, avocado oil, macadamia oil, flaxseed oil
Conventional milk, light and skim varieties	Unpasteurized full cream milk, coconut milk, almond milk or other nut milk
Conventional eggs and meat	Free range and/or grass-fed lean varieties
White bread	Organic sourdough bread, wholemeal and seeded breads, puffed rice cakes or corn cakes, nori sheets (can use as wraps)
White sugar and refined/artificial sweeteners	Honey, pure maple syrup, stevia, coconut sugar, medjool dates
White flour	Organic unbleached flour, spelt flour, coconut flour, almond meal
Table salt	Sea salt, himalayan pink salt, celtic sea salt
Sugary drinks	Fresh smoothies, freshly squeezed juices, lime/lemon in soda water

Processed sauces, dressing and/or marinades	Fresh home-made varieties
Conventional cereal	Oats, buckwheat, quinoa porridge, chia seed pudding, bircher muesli, granola

Hot Tip For Week 2:

Continue to take stock of what you already have available at home and adjust your shopping list accordingly. You will start to notice that there are many similar and repetitive ingredients you will use while eating a Mediterranean Diet. You may have leftover ingredients from last week's shop so ensure you cross those off your list. Buy only the foods you require for the week ahead and ensure you store them correctly to preserve shelf life.

Suggestions on adjusting to a new way of eating and coping with cravings:

- A new way of eating can be exciting. You may be feeling positive; however, we understand it may not always be easy. You may have already struggled with curbing your appetite and cravings. In these moments it's best to have an established game plan. We suggest you write a list of some alternative actions you can choose from instead of succumbing to temptation in moments of weakness. Write a list and stick it on your fridge and when you feel you may be struggling and want to gobble on something that may not benefit your health, pick an action from your list to do instead. Here are some ideas:

  - Make a cup of herbal tea and sip on it in the sunshine

  - Distract yourself by keeping busy – do some gardening, start a project, set out a list of tasks/goals you would like to achieve and make a start on them.

  - Go for a walk

  - Call a friend

  - Take a bath

Whatever it is you may come up with, the idea is to create a practical list of things to do to help replace old unhealthy habits.

- This week, let's introduce Lemon Water. This healthy concoction alkalizes your body and helps flush out toxins. Moreover, it boosts your metabolism and "resets" your appetite. Some say that it even curbs sugar cravings. All you need to do is to squeeze half of a lemon in a glass of water and drink it first thing in the morning.

- Eat regularly and mindfully. Sticking to a meal plan and keeping clear of foods that aren't going to do you any favors is easier when you eat regularly throughout the day. Try and eat your meals at the same time each day and learn to eat mindfully, meaning you're aware and in the moment. Focus on what's happening right now and enjoy food with all your senses. Turn off your cell phone, TV, and laptop. Sit down and savor your meals. It is also important to learn to recognize the difference between physical and emotional hunger. Don't eat when you're stressed, angry, or bored. Keep yourself distracted (refer to your list) until those feelings go away. Your emotions can influence appetite.

This Week's Goal:

1. Take stock of your pantry and start a list of the "simple healthy swaps" you can begin to make in the weeks ahead.

2. Create your list of alternative activities for when you may be struggling through a craving or struggling with "emotional" eating, and stick it on your fridge.

3. Each mealtime, ensure you take the time to enjoy your foods' flavors, colors, and textures and not to rush through every bite.

Final Word:

Don't forget to continue to have fun. Prepare what you can ahead of time to take the stress and chaos out of mealtimes. Don't forget food is not your enemy. It's fuel for your mind and body. Whole, natural foods provide you with the energy needed to function at your peak.

Shrimp and Asparagus Salad

Week 2

Sunday	Monday	Tuesday	Wednesday
Tortilla Espanola *(Page 46)* *(Omit the Italian sausage from this recipe for a vegetarian meal – cook as per recipe, just without the sausage)*	Pistachio Olive Bread *(Page 40)* Serve with feta cheese, sliced olives, and a drizzle of olive oil	Golden Millet Porridge *(Page 32)*	Gourmet Feta Toast *(Page 34)*
Shrimp and Asparagus Salad *(Page 66)*	Portuguese Chorizo Soup *(Page 98)*	Sicilian Eggplant Caponata *(Page 68)* Serve on Pistachio Olive Bread *(Page 40)* *(Make enough of the caponata to have leftovers for Thursday's lunch, store in fridge)*	Leftover Tuscan White Bean Stew *(Page 106)*
Mediterranean Meatballs *(Page 92)*	Spinach Torta *(Page 72)* Serve with Simple Greek Salad *(Page 54)* *(Reheat the leftover spinach torta from last week's Sunday Meal Plan)*	Tuscan White Bean Stew *(Page 106)* *(Make enough to have leftovers for tomorrow's lunch)*	Chicken Piccata *(Page 82)* *(For the demi-glace in this recipe, use chicken stock, unless you have demi-glace to use)*

Notes:

Prepare and cook the Pistachio Olive Bread ready for the week ahead. Depending on servings required you may need to do a double batch as you will need enough for one breakfast and two lunch meals.

Take both the Spinach Torta and Portuguese Soup from the freezer from last week and place in the fridge to defrost.

If you are after a quick and easy lunch tomorrow, you can also prepare the caponata tonight to be ready for Tuesday's lunch. Store in an airtight container in the fridge.

Week 2

Thursday	Friday	Saturday
Overnight Breakfast Strata *(Page 38)*	Breakfast Fig Smoothie *(Page 22)*	Easy Breakfast Pizza *(Page 28)*
Leftover Sicilian Eggplant Caponata *(Page 68)*	Tuna Stuffed Eggplants *(Page 74)* *(Use grated parmesan cheese for the grated cheese in this recipe unless you have other grated cheese on hand you would prefer)*	Leftover Cheese & Spinach Dumplings *(Page 52)*
Fish In Island Sauce *(Page 86)*	Cheese & Spinach Dumplings *(Page 52)* *(Make enough to have leftovers for tomorrow's lunch)*	Falafels in Tortillas with Tahini Sauce *(Page 84)*

Notes:

Tonight's dinner is Cheese & Spinach Dumplings. You will serve these topped with Sun-dried Tomato and Basil Sauce with a sprinkle of feta and/or freshly grated parmesan cheese. Garnish with some fresh basil leaves and season with salt and pepper.

Tomorrow's lunch requires cooked quinoa. To save time tomorrow, cook a batch of quinoa (according to packet directions) tonight and store in the fridge to use tomorrow.

Make time today to make a double batch of the Cottage Cheese Blueberry Casserole. It is on the menu Sunday and Tuesday for breakfast and needs to be made ahead of time.

It's Saturday night, treat yourself to a glass or two of wine and a square of dark chocolate.

WEEK 2 – Shopping List

Vegetables:
Arugala Leaves
Asparagus
Avocados
Butternut Squash
Cabbage
Celery Stalks
Eggplants
Fresh Spinach
Frozen Spinach
Garlic Cloves
Greek Olives
Green Olives
Green Pepper
Kale
Lettuce
Mushrooms
Olives
Onions
Potatoes
Red Bell Pepper
Scallions
Stringed Green Beans
Sundried Tomatoes
Zucchini

Fruit:
Apple
Cherry Tomatoes
Fresh Figs
Frozen Bananas
Lemons
Pomegranate Arils
Tomatoes

Herbs:
Basil
Bay Leaf
Cilantro
Dried Thyme
Italian Dried Herbs
Italian Parsley
Oregano
Parsley

Dairy:
Butter
Cream Cheese
Eggs
Feta
Grated Cheese
Greek Feta
Greek Yogurt
Milk
Mozzarella Cheese
Natural Greek Yogurt
Parmesean Cheese
Ricotta Cheese

Bakery:
Bread Crumbs
Pie Crust
Sourdough Bread
Toast
Tortillas

Meat:
Anchovy Fillets
Chicken Breasts
Chorizo
Ground Beef
Ground Pork
Italian Sausage
Prosciutto
Shrimp

Other:
Almonds
Chia Seeds
Chicken Broth
Chicken Stock
Flaxseed Sprouts
Oats
Pasta
Pepitas
Pine Nuts
Pistachios
Raisins
Walnuts
Worcestershire Sauce

Check Your Pantry For The Following:
Baking Powder
Black Pepper
Canned Chickpeas
Canned Crushed Tomatoes
Canned Diced Tomatoes
Canned Italian Plum
  Tomatoes
Canned Tuna
Canned White Beans
Capers
Celery Seed
Dijon Mustard
Dried Chili Flakes
Dried Mustard
Dried Oregano Leaves
Flour
Garlic Powder
Ground Cinnamon
Ground Cumin
Honey
Mayonnaise
Millet
Nutmeg
Olive Oil
Paprika
Pimento, Jar
Prepared Horseradish
Salt
Sea Salt
Self-Rising Flour
Sugar
Tahini (Sesame Paste)
White Wine Vinegar

Alcohol Used For Cooking:
White Wine

Pistachio and Olive Bread

Mediterranean
Meal Plan

Week 3

Cottage Cheese Blueberry Casserole

Introduction

Welcome to Week 3 of your Mediterranean Meal Plan. We trust that you can start to reap the many benefits this program has to offer.

As you will now begin to learn and also experience, a healthy diet can have a noticeable effect on both how you feel physically, and also how you feel emotionally. A natural, low-processed diet such as the Mediterranean Diet will reduce levels of inflammation which in turn will make you feel great, increase your quality of life and reduce the risk of many chronic diseases.

Introduction to Inflammation—Don't shoot the messenger!

When something harmful or irritating affects our body, the body generates an immune response to try and protect itself and remove the culprit—this is inflammation. The presence of inflammation makes a person susceptible to illness and disease and often occurs years before it becomes apparent. There are a number of factors that cause inflammation, poor diet being the number one!

It is important to take the time and note any ailments you may have had previously or are currently experiencing. Sometimes we may forget or have not taken notice of what may be bothering us.

ACTION:

Take time NOW to listen to and recognise what your body is saying! Furthermore, start to listen to what your body is telling you after EVERY time you eat. It can be these signs that are telling us what foods are causing inflammation, leading to "DIS-Ease" in the body. For example, do you get a runny nose after having dairy, feel tired after gluten, have stomach cramps or feel bloated after wheat, mood swings after sugary drinks......? It is up to YOU to listen to your body and it is important to be aware of what your indicators are when inflammation occurs. Becoming aware of these things will allow you to choose the foods your body can tolerate, allowing you to live a life of vitality and longevity.

Inflammation left unattended to in the body can lead to numerous, serious and debilitating diseases. We don't want that now, do we?

Take note of any symptoms you have had or currently experiencing:

- Bloating
- Reflux
- Heartburn
- Constipation
- Diarrhea
- Irritable Bowel
- Mood Swings

- Hot Flushes
- Tiredness/Fatigue
- Headaches/Migraines
- Aching Joints
- Muscle Cramps
- Sore Back
- Sore Knees

- Fluid Retention
- Flaky/Itchy Skin
- Excess Mucus
- Throat Irritation
- Coughing after eating
- Constant clearing of throat

- _____
- _____
- _____
- _____
- _____
- _____

Recommendations for reducing or eliminating inflammatory foods:

When eating a diet rich in nutrient dense foods as previously outlined, you will find that nutritionally barren food and inflammatory foods will naturally start to fade from your daily eating regime. It is important, however, to know what foods to reduce to a minimum or eliminate. It is important to find out which foods may cause you inflammation and generate irritating or harmful effects on the body. Here are some recommendations and suggestions:

- For most people dairy is highly inflammatory, and yet it can form a large part of people's diet. Foods such as cheese, milk, yogurt (don't forget the milk in your coffee or tea) can be present in almost every meal of the day. If you experience symptoms such as mucus, asthma, allergies, joint pain, nerve pain, arthritis or hay fever while consuming dairy, this may mean dairy is not for you. Signs like these can indicate your immune system has become overburdened. An over-consumption of dairy can be a cause of these inflammatory triggers. It is best to reduce consumption and choose better sources such as plain natural yogurt or kefir and unpasteurized fresh full cream milk.

- Wheat is another food that can be highly inflammatory, with many people finding they are intolerant. This is more due to how it is grown, harvested and processed in today's modern age. If you find wheat is irritating for you it is best to eliminate or reduce significantly in your diet.

  - When choosing a bread try and eat only preservative-free bread, especially no 282. You could also try rye bread or spelt bread—just make sure it is wheat free. Better yet, make your own with quality ingredients.

  - Avoid conventional breakfast cereals as well as cakes, muffins, biscuits, store-bought sandwiches, pies and pastries. These types of foods not only contain wheat, they will also be filled with many other inflammatory ingredients such as refined sugar, vegetable oil and preservatives. For a treat, aim for homemade varieties or, when out look for a gluten-free option where possible.

- Reduce the consumption of any processed foods, including deli meats, bottled sauces, TV dinners, pre-prepared meals, packet soups, noodles, pre-made marinades, chips,etc. Prioritize eliminating packaged purchasing; make what you can yourself from real ingredients.

- Avoid soft drinks, cordials, flavored milks, store-bought fruit juice, iced teas, energy drinks, etc. These drinks are very high in sugar. Drink plenty of water each day, a minimum of two liters.

- Limit caffeinated drinks such as coffee and tea to one to two cups per day and aim to have them no later than 12pm. Try and introduce fruit teas, green tea or herbal teas as an alternative option which you can enjoy as much as you like and have any time of the day.

- If consuming alcohol, try not to consume more than one drink each day on average. Aim to have at least two alcohol-free days per week; this will assist your body with removing any stored toxins. When choosing an alcoholic beverage look for pure distilled varieties such as a good quality vodka or gin. Where you can choose organic and/or preservative-free wines.

Hot Tip For Week 3:

Start learning to read labels on all the items too difficult to (or that you don't have the time to) make yourself and you need to purchase. General rule of thumb is that if you can't recognize an ingredient, chances are your body won't either and won't know how to process it, which may lead to an inflammatory response. Select the product/brand with the least amount of ingredients and that seems to use the most "real" natural foods.

This Week's Goals:

1. Take note of any/all inflammatory responses or conditions you may have experienced/ suffered in the past. Start a food diary and list any triggers that occur after a particular meal and see if a pattern starts to develop. For example, do you feel bloated after each time you eat wheat or do you get a sudden case of the sneezes after you have had some dairy?

2. Take a look in your fridge and pantry and get familiar with your labels. Take some time out and go ahead and read what is in your products. Are there any surprises?

Final Word:

Don't forget that the most powerful tool to overcome inflammation comes from the foods we eat. Choosing the right foods will significantly reduce your risk of illness and chronic disease while ensuring you feel great! Consistently picking the foods that trigger inflammatory responses (don't forget, your body will tell you which ones) can accelerate inflammatory processes in the body leaving you susceptible to disease.

Week 3

Sunday	Monday	Tuesday	Wednesday
Cottage Cheese Blueberry Casserole *(Page 26)*	Golden Millet Porridge *(Page 32)*	Cottage Cheese Blueberry Casserole *(Page 26)*	Spanish Breakfast Beans *(Page 42)* **(Make double the amount required so that you can serve again on Friday)*
Tuscany Sausage & Bean Soup *(Page 78)*	Overnight Breakfast Strata *(Page 38)* **(Prepared last night. Ensure that the leftovers are stored well for Wednesday's lunch)*	Tuscan White Bean Stew *(Page 106)* **(Using leftovers from last night's dinner)*	Overnight Breakfast Strata *(Page 38)* **(Reheat leftovers from Monday)*
Orange Baked Fish with Onions & Mushrooms *(Page 96)*	Tuscan White Bean Stew *(Page 106)* **(Make double the amount required to serve leftovers at lunch tomorrow)*	Chicken Piccata *(Page 82)*	Roasted Lamb Rack with Velvet Black Olive Sauce *(Page 100)*

Notes:

If you have limited time in the mornings, you will want to make tomorrow's breakfast meal tonight so that you can simply reheat in the morning. Don't forget to make double as the Spanish Breakfast Beans will be served twice this week.

Week 3

Thursday	Friday	Saturday
Caprese Breakfast Tart *(Page 24)*	Leftover Spanish Breakfast Beans *(Page 42)* **(Use leftovers from Wednesday's breakfast)*	Fig Smoothie *(Page 22)*
Tuscan Tuna Salad *(Page 76)*	Leftover Caprese Breakfast Tart *(Page 42)*	Tuna Stuffed Eggplants *(Page 74)*
Portuguese Chorizo Soup *(Page 98)*	Stuffed Baked Squid *(Page 102)*	Turkey Barley Soup *(Page 104)*

Notes:

Don't forget to go over this week's goals and action points. Have you noticed your body trying to tell you anything when it comes to the food you eat? Take your time, tune in and start to listen to the messages your body is sending to you.

WEEK 3 – Shopping List

Vegetables:
Arugala Leaves
Bell Pepper
Butternut Squash
Cabbage
Capers
Carrots
Celery Stalk
Cucumber
Eggplants
Garlic
Garlic Cloves
Green Bell Pepper
Green Pepper
Kale
Mushrooms
Nicoise Olives
Olives
Onions
Pearl Onions
Potato
Red Onions
Shallots
String Green Beans
Zucchini

Fruit:
Apple
Blueberries
Currants
Figs
Frozen Bananas
Lemons
Tomatoes

Herbs:
Bay Leaf
Dried Italian Herbs
Dried Marjoram
Dried Thyme
Fresh Basil
Fresh Dill
Fresh Mint
Italian Parsley
Oregano

Parsley
Rosemary Sprig

Dairy:
Butter
Butter (Unsalted)
Cottage Cheese
Eggs
Feta
Milk
Mozzarella
Natural Greek Yogurt
Parmesan Cheese
Sour Cream

Bakery:
Bread Crumbs
Crusty Bread
Sheet Puff Pastry
Sourdough Bread

Meat:
Anchovy Fillets
Chicken Breasts
Chorizo Sausage
Flounder (Fish)
Ground Pork
Italian Sausages
Lamb Racks
Squid
Turkey Breast

Other:
Almonds
Beef Stock
Canned Chickpeas
Canned Diced Tomatoes
Canned Tuna
Chia Seeds
Chicken Broth
Chicken Stock
Honey
Lemon Juice
Millet
Monkfruit Sweetener

Oats
Orange Juice
Pasta
Pine Nuts
Raisins
Rice (Long Grain)
Tomato Sauce
Vegetable Stock
Walnuts
Worcestershire Sauce

**Check Your Pantry For
The Following:**
Almond Extract
Black Pepper
Black Peppercorns
Canned Cannellini Beans
Canned Crushed Tomatoes
Canned Pinto Beans
Canned White Beans
Dried Chili Flakes
Flour
Garlic Powder
Ground Cinnamon
Honey
Italian Dressing
Olive Oil
Paprika
Pearl Barley
Pimentos, Jar
Salt
Sazon
Sea Salt
Sofrito
Spelt Flour
Tomato Pureé
Vanilla Extract

**Alcohol Used For
Cooking:**
Curacao Liqueur
Madeira Wine
Red Wine (Dry)
White Wine

Spanish Breakfast Beans

Mediterranean
Meal Plan

Chicken Pic

Introduction

Welcome to Week 4 of your Mediterranean Meal Plan. This week we are going to discuss food as fuel for our bodies.

When you embark on a new journey of healthy eating you may come across words such as "micronutrients" and "macronutrients". It's a good idea to become familiar with and understand what these actually are, in order to understand what healthy eating, is all about and to find a good balance for yourself.

Basically, our body needs nutrients to grow and thrive. Food essentially (and simply) is fuel for our bodies and it is important we are filling our bodies with the right type of fuel it requires.

When we consume food, our bodies convert it into a source we can use; for example, a protein is converted into amino acids which are the building blocks to make muscle, bone, tissue and skin.

Healthy fats are needed to maintain good health, create strong healthy cells and support good brain function. Carbohydrates are turned into glucose which supplies our cells with energy; however, our general diet can consist of too many carbs with the excess glucose being stored as fat. Fresh fruits and vegetables support our immune system and provide our bodies with the vitamins and minerals required for good health.

Considerations on what foods to select at each meal:

Our bodies need the right balance of the right fuel to perform at their best, just like a car needs to be given the appropriate fuel to drive. When selecting the foods (fuel) you will have at each meal, take into consideration the following:

1. Incorporate living foods (such as vegetables/fruits/herbs/seeds/spices) in every meal of the day. These will support your overall health and well-being by providing an array of vitamins, minerals and antioxidants. Living foods (mainly vegetables) should make up roughly half of your plate.

2. Incorporate a protein portion in every meal of the day. Opt for plant-based protein sources as best you can; otherwise choose lean varieties of meat and seafood. Quality sources of protein should make up roughly one quarter of your plate.

3. Look at replacing refined carbohydrates such as white pasta/white bread with wholemeal/wholegrain varieties. Wholemeal sources will provide longer lasting energy along with more nutritional value. Complex carbohydrates should make up roughly one quarter of your plate.

4. Add a serving of a healthy oil/fat in every meal of the day, such as a drizzle of olive oil over a salad or a sprinkle of flaxseeds on top of a meal.

Living Foods—The Essential Focus of the Mediterranean Diet

Vegetables, fruits, nuts and seeds are full of vitamins and minerals which make our body work properly, boost the immune system, support normal growth and development, and help cells and organs do their jobs. Many people today are deficient in an array of nutrients; therefore, it is important that plenty of local, fresh and seasonal fruits and vegetables are incorporated into a daily diet.

Recommendations for daily intake of vitamins and minerals:

1. Eat five to nine handfuls of a wide range of vegetables per day, or as much as possible. Include lots of different colors, e.g., mushrooms, cauliflower, bell peppers, tomatoes, leeks, garlic, carrots, etc.

2. Have up to two pieces of fruit per day (no more while trying to lose weight). Sample a good variety of fruits such as berries, citrus, banana, melons, etc.

3. Limit fruit at breakfast while trying to lose weight. Opt for a high-protein breakfast which will keep you full for longer and also balance blood sugar.

4. Buy fruit and vegetables only when in season. Also try to buy local ripe fruit where possible; look into farmers markets. You will get more nutrients (and flavor) when purchasing in season, local, ripe produce.

5. Eat raw fruits and vegetables as much as possible. Up to 30% of vitamins can be lost in cooking.

6. Aim to include a bowl of green leafy veggies in your daily diet. Please note lettuce has poor nutrition content so it is better to choose dark leafy greens like spinach, watercress and arugula.

7. Cruciferous vegetables such as cauliflower, broccoli, cabbage, spinach, kale, bok choy, brussels sprouts (and similar green leafy vegetables) should be the basis of your veggie intake. They are high in vitamins, soluble fiber and contain many nutrients and phytochemicals which protect against disease. It is thought that cruciferous vegetables are actually better eaten cooked (rather than raw).

8. Potato, pumpkin and sweet potato are high in carbohydrates. Limit your intake unless you have a high exercise level.

9. While nuts and seeds are a good source of protein and fat, they also provide a wide variety of nutrients. Incorporate them into your daily diet by eating them fresh, raw and unsalted; however, watch the amount you consume as they are very high in calories. Restrict when you are trying to lose weight.

Final thoughts:

Developing a healthy diet incorporates eating a good balance of macro-nutrients such as protein, carbohydrates and healthy fats which we will cover in more detail over the following weeks.

Our bodies need the right balance of the right fuel to perform at their best. Selecting the right foods will have you living an optimized life.

Living foods that are bursting with vitamins, minerals and antioxidants are essential for good overall health and well-being. They should make up the largest part of our daily diets.

Pickled Herring with Beet Dip Crostini

Week 4

Sunday	Monday	Tuesday	Wednesday
Breakfast Fig Smoothie *(Page 22)*	Leftover Neapolitan Polenta Pie *(Page 94)* *(Use leftovers from last night's dinner, simply reheat and serve)*	Golden Millet Porridge *(Page 32)*	Gourmet Feta Toast *(Page 34)*
Carpaccio *(Page 50)*	Rice & Lentil Salad *(Page 62)* *(Make double the amount required to serve on Wednesday for lunch)*	Pickled Herring with Beet Dip Crostini *(Page 58)*	Rice & Lentil Salad *(Page 62)* *(Using leftovers from Monday. Simply serve cold)*
Neapolitan Polenta Pie *(Page 94)* *(Make double the amount required for leftovers for tomorrow's breakfast)*	Chicken Piccata *(Page 82)*	Fish in Island Sauce *(Page 86)*	Meatloaf Stuffed with Proscuitto & Cheese *(Page 90)*

Notes:

Week 4

Thursday	Friday	Saturday
Breakfast Fig Smoothie *(Page 22)*	Golden Millet Porridge *(Page 32)*	Gourmet Feta Toast *(Page 34)*
Pickled Herring with Beet Dip Crostini *(Page 58)*	Turkey Barley Soup *(Page 104)* *(Simply reheat leftovers from last night and serve)*	Tortilla Espanola *(Page 46)*
Turkey Barley Soup *(Page 104)* *(Use chicken if desired. Make double the amount to enjoy it again Friday for lunch)*	Mediterranean Meatballs *(Page 92)*	Orange Baked Fish with Onions & Mushrooms *(Page 96)*

Notes:

It's Saturday night, time to enjoy a glass or two of wine and a couple of squares of dark chocolate.

WEEK 4 – Shopping List

Vegetables:
Arugala Leaves
Avocado
Beets
Butternut Squash
Capers
Carrots
Celery Stalks
Dried Porcini Mushrooms
Eggplant
Field Mushrooms
Garlic Clove
Green Bell Pepper
Mushrooms
Onions
Pearl Onions
Potatoes
Red Bell Pepper
Red Onion
Scallions
Shallots
Spanish Onion
Yellow Bell Pepper
Zucchini

Fruit:
Apple
Figs
Frozen Bananas
Lemon
Pomegranate Arils
Tomatoes

Herbs:
Basil
Bay Leaf
Dried Italian Herbs
Dried Majoram
Dried Oregano
Dried Tarragon
Dried Thyme
Mint
Parsley

Dairy:
Butter
Eggs
Greek Feta
Mozzarella Cheese
Natural Greek Yogurt
Parmesan Cheese

Bakery:
Bread
Bread Crumbs
Crostini
Toast

Meat:
Beef Fillet
Chicken Breasts
Fish Fillets
Flounder (Fish)
Ground Beef
Italian Sausage
Prosciutto
Turkey Breast

Other:
Almonds
Canned Chickpeas
Canned Green Lentils
Chia Seeds
Chicken Stock
Flaxseed Sprouts
Gherkins
Lemon Juice
Millet
Oats
Orange Juice
Pasta
Pepitas
Pizza Sauce
Raisins
Rice
Walnuts

Check Your Pantry For The Following:
Apple Cider Vinegar
Black Pepper
Canned Diced Tomatoes
Canned Tomato Soup
Dry Mustard
Fennel Seed
Flour
Ground Cinnamon
Honey
Labna
Nutmeg
Olive Oil
Paprika
Pearl Barley
Pickled Herring
Polenta
Prepared Mustard
Salt
Sea Salt
White Wine Vinegar

Alcohol Used For Cooking:
Curacao Liqueur
Red Wine
White Wine

Breakfast Fig Smoothie

45

Mediterranean
Meal Plan

Week

5

Stuffed Mushrooms

Introduction

Welcome to Week 5 of your Mediterranean Meal Plan. This week we are placing a spotlight on healthy fats, which are an important focus of the Mediterranean Diet.

Healthy fats and oils are an essential part of a healthy diet (one of three macronutrients). They also help assist with satiety (keeping us feeling full for longer) as well as reducing cravings. The Mediterranean Diet features many sources of quality fats such as olives, olive oil, nuts, seeds, avocado and fatty fish.

With our cell walls being made of both protein and oil, healthy fats and oils have an important role in maintaining good health, keeping our cell walls healthy and strong. This is most noticeable in our skin and hair. Oils also contain vitamins to support our brain, making it work properly.

The problem many people face is consuming the wrong kind of oils and fats which can lead to inflammation (as discussed last week), putting them at risk of illness and disease.

Some sources of healthy oils and fats included in the Mediterranean Diet are:

- Cold-pressed olive oil
- Coconut oil
- Avocado oil
- Macadamia oil
- Flaxseed oil
- Avocados, olives, coconut, nuts and seeds
- Grass-fed butter and ghee
- Salmon and ground flaxseeds are great sources of omega-3!

Recommendations for daily fats and oils intake:

- Ensure you have a serving of healthy fats/oils in every meal of the day. You can do this by having half an avocado with breakfast or coconut and ground flaxseeds in a morning smoothie. Lunch could include nuts and seeds in a salad with an olive oil dressing, and at dinner time you can cook your meat in either grass-fed ghee or coconut oil, served with a little homemade mayonnaise.

- Aim to include avocados, coconuts, flaxseeds, a variety of nuts and seeds, olives and salmon regularly in your diet.

- Ensure the correct use of your oils to protect from free radicals. Use coconut oil and ghee for cooking at high heats, olive oil for medium heat or served at room temperature, and avocado oil, macadamia nut oil and flaxseed oil as dressings over a meal.

- Stop any use of toxic man-made oils such as margarine, canola oil and other vegetable oils. These oils are highly inflammatory due to the way they have been processed/ made. Simply swap with healthier alternatives such as olive oil.

- Reduce the use of animal fats by buying lean cuts of meat. Toxins can be stored in animal fat.

- When cooking, use methods such as steaming, poaching and grilling rather than frying.

This Week's Goals:

1. Take stock of any man-made oils such as margarine and vegetable oil. Are there oils you can start to replace with a healthier alternative? Make a list and once you run out and need to replace an item, source a quality, healthier alternative.

2. Create a list of healthy snacks that are a good source of quality fats. Some ideas are olives, avocado dip, trail mix and flaxseed crackers. Opt for these snacks between meals if you are feeling hungry.

Final Thoughts:

Don't forget, quality fats as we have outlined are not bad and will not have a negative effect on your health. Instead they will help combat inflammation, provide long-lasting energy and give you glowing skin, shiny hair and strong nails. Make "fat" your friend.

Breakfast Pizza

Week 5

Sunday	Monday	Tuesday	Wednesday
Stuffed Mushrooms *(Page 44)*	Breakfast Fig Smoothie *(Page 22)*	Easy Breakfast Pizza *(Page 29)*	Plain Greek Yogurt with Fresh Berries *(Page 138)*
Tuscan White Bean Stew *(Page 106)*	Spinach Torta *(Page 72)*	Leftover Tuscany Sausage & Bean Soup *(Page 78)* *(Simply reheat leftover soup from last night's dinner)*	Spinach Torta *(Page 72)* *(Make double the amount required for lunch on Friday. Store leftovers, wrapped and in the fridge)*
Grilled Salmon on Herbed Couscous *(Page 64)*	Tuscany Sausage & Bean Soup *(Page 78)* *(Make a double batch to serve as leftovers for tomorrow's lunch))*	Tuna Stuffed Eggplants *(Page 74)*	Fregula with Clams & Chilis *(Page 88)*

Notes:

If you are pressed for time tomorrow, make the Spinach Torta today. It will be ready to serve for lunch tomorrow. Take note though, you will need to make triple the amount so you can enjoy it three times this week.

Week 5

Thursday	Friday	Saturday
Breakfast Fig Smoothie *(Page 22)*	Plain Greek Yogurt with Fresh Berries *(Page 138)*	Lemon Ricotta Pancakes *(Page 36)*
Sicilian Eggplant Caponata *(Page 68)*	Leftover Spinach Torta *(Page 72)* *(Reuse leftovers from Wednesday; serve cold or reheat to serve hot)*	Chickpea Salad *(Page 132)*
Grilled Salmon On Herbed Couscous *(Page 64)*	Meatloaf Stuffed with Proscuitto & Cheese *(Page 90)*	Chicken Piccata *(Page 82)*

Notes:

It's Saturday night, time to enjoy a glass or two of wine and a couple of squares of dark chocolate.

WEEK 5 – Shopping List

Vegetables:
Arugala Leaves
Bell Pepper
Cabbage
Capers
Carrots
Celery Stalk
Chives
Eggplants
Frozen Spinach
Garlic Cloves
Green Bell Peppers
Green Olives
Mushrooms
Olives
Onions
Portobello Mushrooms
Red Onions
Yellow Bell Pepper
Zucchinis

Fruit:
Blueberries
Figs
Frozen Bananas
Lemons
Raspberries
Strawberries
Sundried Tomatoes
Tomatoes

Herbs:
Basil
Bay Leaf
Dried Oregano
Italian Dried Herbs
Italian Parsley
Mint
Oregano
Parsley
Thyme

Dairy:
Butter
Cream Cheese
Eggs
Feta
Milk
Mozzarella Cheese
Natural Greek Yogurt
Parmesan Cheese
Plain Greek Yogurt
Ricotta Cheese

Bakery:
Bread Crumbs
Pie Crust

Meat:
Anchovy Fillets
Chicken Breasts
Ground Beef
Italian Sausages
Prosciutto
Salmon Fillets
Tiny Clams

Other:
Almonds
Beef Stock
Canned Chickpeas
Canned Italian Plum
  Tomatoes
Canned Tuna
Chia Seeds
Chicken Broth
Chicken Stock
Couscous
Lemon Juice
Lemon Verbena
Oatmeal
Steel Cut Oats
Pasta
Pine Nuts
Tomato Purée
Vegetable Stock

Check Your Pantry For The Following:
Baking Powder
Black Pepper
Canned Cannellini Beans
Canned Crushed Tomatoes
Canned White Beans
Cumin
Dijon Mustard
Dried Chili Flakes
Flour
Garlic Powder
Honey
Olive Oil
Paprika
Prepared Mustard
Red Wine Vinegar
Saffron
Salt
Sea Salt
Self-Rising Flour
Sugar
Tomato Soup
White Wine Vinegar
Whole Wheat Flour

Alcohol Used For Cooking:
White Wine (Dry)

Tuna Stuffed Eggplants

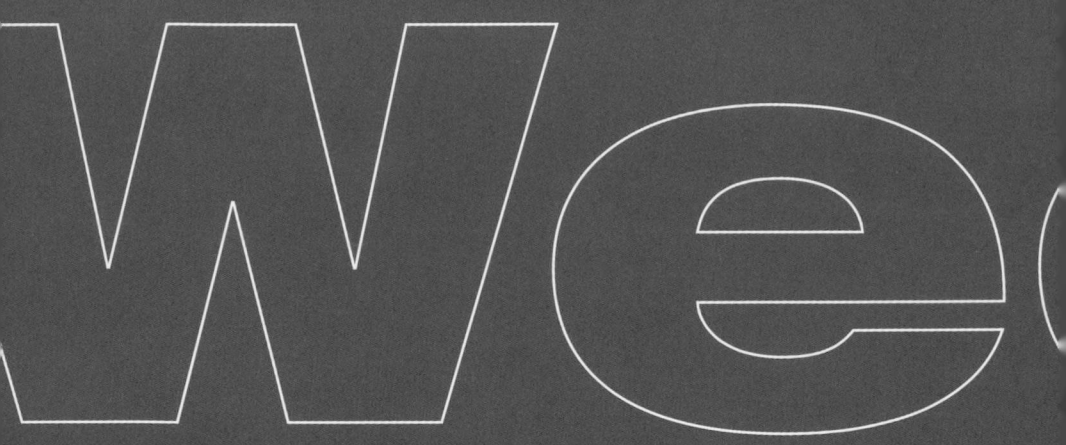

Mediterranean
Meal Plan

Week

6

Overnight Breakfast Strata

Introduction

Welcome to Week 6 of your Mediterranean Meal Plan. This week we are taking the time to understand carbohydrates and how to incorporate them into our daily diet in a healthy way.

Carbohydrates provide our body energy through glucose, the main fuel for our body. The standard western diet is generally high in carbohydrates which for some people can present risks such as obesity and type 2 diabetes.

While carbohydrates are an essential part of a healthy diet, don't forget that not all carbs are created equal. It is best to choose healthy sources of carbs such as low glycemic index whole grains, fruits and vegetables. When choosing carbs, we want to ensure the carbohydrates we are consuming have a slow absorption rate that promotes natural insulin levels rather than drastic insulin spikes. Insulin is the hormone that is essentially used for fat storage. Choosing the wrong carbs as well as a high intake of carbs can contribute dramatically to weight gain.

Some examples of "good" whole, complex carbs that you should consider incorporating in your daily diet:

- Vegetables

- Fruits

- Legumes, such as lentils, chickpeas, kidney beans, etc.

- Nuts and seeds

- Whole grains, such as oats, quinoa, brown rice, buckwheat, spelt, etc.

Recommendations For Daily Carbohydrate Intake:

1. Limit to low glycemic index and wholemeal sources such as brown rice, buckwheat, pumpkin and sweet potato.

2. While trying to lose weight your carb intake should be very restricted. Only have small servings as necessary at mealtimes, such as half a potato or 1/3 cup of steamed brown rice.

3. Limit, as much as possible, processed, refined, high GI carbs such as sugar, refined breads, cakes and pastries, pasta, sugary drinks and most store-bought breakfast cereals. These foods are low in fiber and provide no nutritional value. They may give you a quick burst of energy but will then leave you feeling tired and lethargic soon after.

4. Your intake should match your energy output. If you live an active lifestyle and exercise often you may find you are able to consume a little more carbs than the rest of us. If you are not regularly physically active your carb intake should be a little lower.

5. Avoid snacking on "carb foods." Aim for snacks that contain protein and/or healthy fats such as nuts and seeds, flaxseed crackers, blissballs made with coconut oil, veggie sticks and hummus.

Final Thoughts:

Don't forget there is not a "one-size-fits-all" plan when it comes to eating healthy, in particular when consuming carbs. Find what works for you and stick to it—just be sure you are choosing nutrient-rich carbs that are low glycemic index and are from whole food sources.

We do suggest, though, that if you are trying to lose weight or may be at risk of type 2 diabetes you may want to look at limiting the amount of carbs you are serving each mealtime.

Sicilian Eggplant Caponata

Week 6

Sunday	Monday	Tuesday	Wednesday
Sun Smoothie *(Page 110)*	Overnight Breakfast Strata *(Page 38)* *(Make double the amount required as you will be serving leftovers for lunch tomorrow)*	Golden Millet Porridge *(Page 32)*	Tortilla Espanola *(Page 46)* *(Use chorizo in place of the Italian sausage as this will already be on your shopping list this week)*
Simple Marinated Chicken Breast *(Page 70)* Served with Simple Greek Salad *(Page 54)*	Sicilian Eggplant Caponata, served on crusty baguette *(Page 68)* *(Make double the amount required to serve for lunch on Wednesday)*	Overnight Breakfast Strata *(Page 38)* *(Leftover from yesterday's breakfast)*	Sicilian Eggplant Caponata, served on crusty baguette *(Page 68)* *(Leftover from Monday)*
Grilled Salmon on Herbed Couscous *(Page 64)*	Falafels in Tortillas with Tahini Sauce *(Page 84)*	Pickled Herring with Beet Dip Crostini *(Page 58)*	Portuguese Chorizo Soup *(Page 98)* *(Ensure you make enough for leftovers to serve at lunch tomorrow)*

Notes:

To save time tomorrow, prepare the Caponata today for tomorrow's lunch. Be sure to make enough for both Monday and Wednesday's lunch.

Tomorrow for breakfast you will be having Overnight Breakfast Strata. As the name suggests, you will be **making this tonight** and storing in the fridge to cook in the morning. **Make double for two meals this week**.

Week 6

Thursday	Friday	Saturday
Golden Millet Porridge *(Page 32)*	Sun Smoothie *(Page 110)*	Tortilla Espanola *(Page 46)* **(Use chorizo in place of the Italian sausage as this will already be on your shopping list this week)*
Portuguese Chorizo Soup *(Page 98)* **(Use leftovers from last night's dinner, simply reheat and serve)*	Shrimp & Asparagus Salad *(Page 66)*	Simple Marinated Chicken Breast *(Page 70)*
Mediterranean Meatballs *(Page 92)*	Mediterranean Meatballs *(Page 92)*	Fish in Island Sauce *(Page 86)*

Notes:

Use dinner leftovers for dinner tomorrow.		You made it! It's Saturday so grab yourself a glass of wine or two and a square of dark chocolate.

WEEK 6 – Shopping List

Vegetables:
Asparagus
Beets
Black-Ripe Olives
Butternut Squash
Capers
Celery
Cherry Tomatoes
Cucumber
Eggplant
Garlic Cloves
Green Olives
Green Pepper
Kale
Lettuce
Mixed Salad Greens
Onion
Potatoes
Red Bell Pepper
Scallions
Shallots
Spanish Onion
Stringed Green Beans
Tomatoes
Yellow Bell Pepper
Zucchini

Fruit:
Apple
Banana

Herbs:
Basil
Bay Leaf
Cilantro
Oregano
Parsley
Tarragon
Thyme

Dairy:
Almond Milk
Eggs
Feta
Labna
Milk
Parmesan Cheese

Bakery:
Bread
Crostini
Sourdough Bread
Tortillas

Meat:
Chicken Breast
Chorizo Sausage
Fish Fillets
Ground Beef
Ground Pork
Italian Sausage
Salmon Fillets
Shrimp

Other:
Couscous
Honey
Lemon Juice
Millet
Orange Juice
Pine Nuts
Tahini
Walnuts

Check Your Pantry For The Following:
Apple Cider Vinegar
Baking Powder
Canned Chickpeas
Canned Diced Tomatoes
Canned Italian Plum
  Tomatoes
Chicken Stock
Cumin
Dry Mustard
Gherkins
Ground Cinnamon
Horseradish
Italian Dressing
Mayonnaise
Nutmeg
Olive Oil
Pepper
Pickled Herring
Pimientos, Jar
Raisins
Salt
Sea Salt
Sugar
Vegetable Stock
Wheat Germ
White Wine Vinegar
Worcestershire Sauce

Tuscan Tuna Salad

Mediterranean Meal Plan

ek7

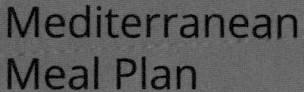

Gourmet Feta Toast

Introduction

Welcome to Week 7 of your Mediterranean Meal Plan. This week we are looking at protein, another macronutrient like carbohydrates and fat.

Protein is an important part of a healthy diet. Studies have actually shown that protein can help improve health in many ways, including lowering blood pressure, combating diabetes as well as weight loss and improving strength. We want to ensure we are consuming a high-quality source of protein at each mealtime.

Protein is a nutrient that is converted into amino acids which are the body's building blocks to make muscle, bone, tissue and skin. We also need amino acids to make enzymes, hormones and even our DNA. Our body does not store a lot of protein, so we must constantly replace it by eating in our diet. Many people today do not get enough protein in their diet and get too many calories from sugar and carbs. If we do not have enough protein in our diet, we start to break down muscle to obtain it.

Some sources of dietary protein include:

- Beans and legumes (such as lentils and chickpeas)
- Lean meat, poultry, fish and other seafood
- Eggs
- Dairy products like milk, yogurt and cheese
- Seeds and nuts

Recommendations for daily protein intake:

1. Have a serving of good quality protein each day from lean chicken, fish or free-range eggs.
2. Make most sources of protein vegetable-based. Lentils, beans, chickpeas, quinoa and chia are all good options. Aim for at least one meatless day each week; however, work towards 3–4 days where your main focus will be on plant-based protein sources. This will give your digestive system a rest, which in turn will support your overall health.
3. Limit red meat to only once or twice per week. Choose lean cuts and preferably wild sources. Red meat is very acidic and can compromise the body's alkaline environment. A high acidic diet can contribute to fatigue, compromise the immune system and make us vulnerable to illness.
4. A serving of protein should be present in every meal each day, such as eggs or natural Greek yogurt for breakfast, nuts, seeds and a sprinkle of feta in a salad for lunch and legumes/beans or lean meat for dinner.

Final Thoughts:

Protein will help support a healthy diet. It can help keep off unwanted weight, reduce the risk and help manage type 2 diabetes and manage blood pressure.

It is important to ensure you are using lean, quality sources and focusing particularly on plant-based varieties to ensure you are reaping the full rewards and health benefits that this amazing nutrient has to offer.

Caprese Breakfast Tart

Week 7

Sunday	Monday	Tuesday	Wednesday
Spanish Breakfast Beans *(Page 42)* *(Make double the amount required to have as leftovers for Tuesday's breakfast)*	Plain Greek Yogurt and Fresh Berries *(Page 138)*	Spanish Breakfast Beans *(Page 42)* *(Use Sunday leftovers)*	Gourmet Feta Toast *(Page 34)*
Caprese Breakfast Tart *(Page 24)*	Tuscan Tuna Salad *(Page 76)*	Spinach Torta *(Page 72)*	Sicilian Eggplant Caponata *(Page 68)*
Chicken Piccata *(Page 82)*	Fish in Island Sauce *(Page 86)*	Sicilian Eggplant Caponata *(Page 68)* *(Make double the amount to have as leftovers for lunch tomorrow)*	Turkey Barley Soup *(Page 104)* *(Make a larger portion that we'll re-use over the coming days)*

Notes:

	Can substitute the fish dinner with leftover tuna from the salad for lunch		Prep the Cottage Cheese Casserole tonight for tomorrow's breakfast to save time in the morning

Week 7

Thursday	Friday	Saturday
Cottage Cheese Blueberry Casserole *(Page 26)* *(Make two full servings to have for breakfast on Saturday)*	Sun Smoothie *(Page 110)*	Cottage Cheese Blueberry Casserole *(Page 26)* *(Use the leftovers from Thursday)*
Turkey Barley Soup *(Page 104)* *(Use the leftovers from last night's dinner)*	Tuscan Tuna Salad *(Page 76)*	Rice & Lentil Salad *(Page 62)*
Spinach Torta *(Page 72)*	Fregola with Clams and Chilis *(Page 88)*	Tuscan White Bean Stew *(Page 106)*

Notes:

	Cook the required rice for tomorrow's lunch and store in an airtight container in the fridge.	Cheers! Grab a glass or two of wine and a couple of squares of dark chocolate to celebrate making it to Saturday!

WEEK 7 – Shopping List

Vegetables:

Arugala
Avocado
Bell Pepper
Cabbage
Capers
Carrots
Celery
Cucumber
Eggplant
Fennel
Garlic
Green Bell Pepper
Green Olives
Olives
Onion
Potatoes
Red Onion
Scallions
Spinach
Tomatoes
Yellow Bell Pepper

Fruit:

Banana
Blueberries
Lemon Lime Wedges
Lemons
Pomegranate
Strawberries

Herbs:

Basil
Bay Leaf
Dried Oregano Leaves
Dry Thyme
Italian Parsley
Italian Dried Herbs
Mint
Parsley
Saffron

Dairy:

Almond Milk
Butter
Cottage Cheese
Eggs
Fresh Mozzarella
Greek Feta
Greek Yogurt
Parmesan
Sour Cream

Bakery:

Crusty Bread
Pie Crust
Sheet Puff Pastry

Meat:

Chicken Breast
Fish Fillets
Prosciutto
Tiny Clams
Turkey Breast

Other:

Chickpeas
Flaxseed Sprouts
Green Lentils
Italian Dressing
Lemon Juice
Monk Fruit Sweetener
Orange Juice
Pepitas
Pine Nuts
Pinto Beans
Sazon
Sofrito

**Check Your Pantry For
The Following:**

Almond Extract
Anchovy Fillets
Black Pepper
Canned Chickpeas
Canned Crushed Tomatoes
Canned Diced Tomatoes

Canned Italian Plum
  Tomatoes
Canned Tuna
Canned White Beans
Chicken Broth
Chicken Stock
Chili Flakes
Dijon Mustard
Dried Marjoram
Flour
Fregola
Garlic Powder
Oatmeal
Olive Oil
Oregano
Paprika
Pasta
Pearl Barley
Rice
Spelt Flour
Sugar
Sundried Tomatoes
Tomato Purée
Tomato Sauce
Vanilla Extract
Vegetable Stock
Wheat Germ
White Wine Vinegar

**Alcohol Used For
Cooking:**

White Wine

Turkey Barley Soup

Wee

Mediterranean
Meal Plan

Carpaccio

Introduction

Congratulations!

You've made it to week 8 and you're heading into your last week.

You now have the information required to reach your health goals and maintain a way of eating that will ensure you thrive.

This program will have provided you a kick start to your journey of living a life of vitality and longevity. You will now have picked up skills such as knowing what foods to select to ensure you are eating for optimal health, creating daily healthy habits and listening to and being in tune with your body.

You may have experienced weight loss, increased energy, clearer skin and other health benefits due to removing nutritionally barren and inflammatory food from your diet and eating a diet rich in the macronutrients that your body is designed for. The long-term benefits of this are significant and now you can look forward to an enhanced quality of life.

Steps Ahead:

Feel free to continue to use this program as a guide to carry on with the same eating habits. You will now notice that the meals each week share similar attributes. This will be the basis of your healthy eating from now on and you can carry on eating this way indefinitely. Let's quickly recap some of the basics to remember and take into account for everyday healthy eating from here on in:

- Have fun! Healthy eating is meant to be enjoyable, exciting and simple. There is no need to stress about it or make things too complicated. Use what ingredients you have available, menu plan and take stock of what you have each week to use.

- Make "real food" swaps with the things you can easily make. Don't forget to pay attention to the ingredients list on packaged food items.

- Prepare what you can ahead of time to take the stress and chaos out of mealtimes. Don't forget food is not your enemy. It's fuel for your mind and body.

- Choosing the right foods will significantly reduce your risk of illness and chronic disease while ensuring you feel great! Consistently picking the foods that trigger inflammatory responses (don't forget, your body will tell you which ones), can accelerate inflammatory processes in the body leaving you susceptible to disease.

- Our bodies need the right balance of the right fuel to perform at their best. Selecting the right foods will have you living an optimized life.

- Living foods that are bursting with vitamins, minerals and antioxidants are essential for good overall health and well-being. They should make up the largest part of our daily diets.

- Don't forget, quality fats are not bad and will not have a negative effect on your health. Instead they will help combat inflammation, provide long lasting energy, give you glowing skin, shiny hair and strong nails. Make "fat" your friend.

- There is not a "one-size-fits-all" plan when it comes to eating healthy, in particular when consuming carbs. Be sure to choose nutrient-rich carbs that are low in GI and from whole food sources.

- Lean, quality protein sources (in particular plant-based varieties) will help support a healthy diet. Protein can help keep off unwanted weight, reduce the risk and help manage type 2 diabetes and manage blood pressure.

Final Thoughts:

The occasional treat is okay, great in fact, as you want to nourish your soul and ensure a healthy relationship with food. A good rule of thumb to abide by is the 80/20 rule. Aim to eat the foods that nurture and nourish your body 80% of the time, while allowing yourself to enjoy the foods that nurture and nourish your soul 20% of the time.

Don't forget this program has taught you how food affects your overall health. If you fall back into old unhealthy habits you will be sure to lose the positive effects of healthy eating that you went to so much effort to achieve.

Golden Millet Porridge

Week 8

Sunday	Monday	Tuesday	Wednesday
Golden Millet Porridge *(Page 32)*	Easy Breakfast Pizza *(Page 28)* *(Make enough for leftovers tomorrow for breakfast)*	Easy Breakfast Pizza *(Page 28)*	Lemon Ricotta Pancakes *(Page 36)*
Turkey Barley Soup *(Page 104)*	Carpaccio *(Page 50)*	Chickpea Salad *(Page 132)*	Mediterranean Hummus Stuffed Peppers *(Page 130)*
Mediterranean Meatballs *(Page 92)*	Stuffed Mushrooms *(Page 44)*	Simple Marinated Chicken Breasts *(Page 70)* *(Save leftovers for dinner tomorrow)*	Simple Marinated Chicken Breasts *(Page 70)*

Notes:

Week 8

Thursday	Friday	Saturday
Golden Millet Porridge *(Page 32)*	Breakfast Fig Smoothie *(Page 22)*	Mediterranean Hummus Stuffed Peppers *(Page 130)*
Carpaccio *(Page 50)*	Cheese & Spinach Dumplings *(Page 52)* *(Make two full servings to have for dinner tomorrow as well)*	Chickpea Salad *(Page 132)*
Turkey Barley Soup *(Page 104))*	Stuffed Mushrooms *(Page 44)*	Cheese & Spinach Dumplings *(Page 52)*

Notes:

WOW! You've completed the full 8-week meal plan challenge! Curate your 9th week (and all weeks afterwards) with some of your favorite recipes that you've tried over the last 8 weeks.

Don't forget to have a couple glasses of wine tonight to celebrate!

WEEK 8 - Shopping List

Vegetables:
Arugala
Bell Peppers
Black Olives
Butternut Squash
Capers
Carrots
Cucumber
Eggplant
Fresh Spinach
Garlic Clove
Green Peppers
Lemons
Mushrooms
Olives
Onions
Portobello Mushrooms
Red Onion
Shallots
Zucchini

Fruit:
Apples
Bananas
Tomatoes

Herbs:
Basil
Bay Leaf
Chives
Lemon Verbena
Parsley

Dairy:
Butter
Cream Cheese
Eggs
Feta
Milk
Parmesan Cheese
Plain Greek Yogurt
Ricotta Cheese

Bakery:
Bread

Meat:
Beef Fillet
Chicken Breast
Ground Beef
Proscuitto
Turkey Breast

Other:
Chickpeas
Hummus
Lemon Juice
Orange Juice

Check Your Pantry For The Following:
Almonds
Baking Powder
Chia Seeds
Chicken Stock
Cumin
Dry Thyme
Dry Marjoram
Figs

Ground Black Pepper
Ground Cinnamon
Honey
Millet
Mustard
Nutmeg
Oats
Olive Oil
Pearl Barley
Plain Flour
Raisins
Red Wine Vinegar
Salt
Sea Salt
Self Rising Flour
Sugar
Sundried Tomatoes
Walnuts
White Wine Vinegar
Whole Wheat Flour

Alcohol Used For Cooking:
Red Wine

uit Salad with Italian Ricotta